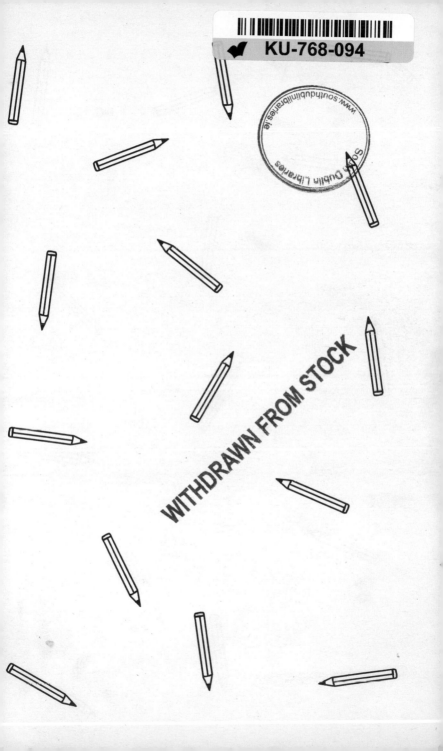

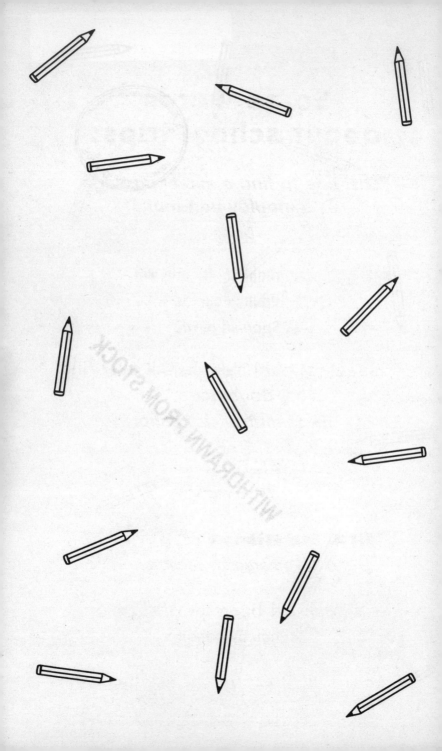

Some words about school trips:

"Last one to find a secret passage is a mouldy banana!"
Daisy

"Aaaaaargghhhh! No one will ever find my doubloons."
A Spanish pirate

"Aaaaaargghhhh! No one will ever find my doubloons."
The Spanish pirate's parrot

"Has anyone seen Daisy and Gabby?"
Mrs Peters

"Fire, ambulance or police?"
The emergency services

"I wish I'd been an orange."
A mouldy banana

More Daisy adventures!

Kes Gray

DAISY

and the trouble with

SCHOOL TRIPS

RED FOX

RED FOX

UK | USA | Canada | Ireland | Australia
India | New Zealand | South Africa

Red Fox is part of the Penguin Random House group of companies
whose addresses can be found at global.penguinrandomhouse.com.

www.penguin.co.uk
www.puffin.co.uk
www.ladybird.co.uk

First published 2018
This edition published 2020

001

Set in VAG Rounded Light 15pt/23pt
Printed in Great Britain by Clays Ltd, Elcograf S.p.A.

A CIP catalogue record for this book is available from the British Library

ISBN: 978-1-782-95971-7

All correspondence to
Red Fox, Penguin Random House Children's
One Embassy Gardens,
8 Viaduct Gardens, London SW11 7BW

To Matt, Amanda, Anna and Lizzie

CHAPTER 1

The **trouble with school trips** is they can get you into trouble.

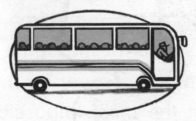

Especially school trips that make you look for secret passages. Secret passages on school trips can be really hard to find, especially if no one has ever found them before. Doubly especially if your teacher has given you a worksheet to fill in while you are looking. And triply especially if your teacher has told you that when you're on the school trip you're meant to be an ambassador for the school. Looking for secret passages at the same time as filling in worksheets at the same time as being an ambassador for the school is about the most impossible thing that anyone could ever be asked to do. In fact, it should be against the law because it didn't just make me get into trouble – it made half my whole entire class get into trouble too. (Not including Barry Morely.) WHICH ISN'T MY FAULT!!!!!

CHAPTER 2

It was about two weeks ago that Mrs Peters first told us that we were going on a school trip. She didn't just tell us. First, she told us to sit down on the floor, sit up straight, fold our arms and get ready for some special news.

"Children," said Mrs Peters, "I'm very pleased to tell you that as part of our local history studies, we will be going on a historical school trip to Bobbington Hall."

"Did she say historical or hysterical?" whispered Gabby.

"Historical, I think," I whispered back.

"Built in the time of Henry the Eighth, Bobbington Hall is a very fine example of an old English country house," said Mrs Peters. "Visiting Bobbington Hall will be a chance for us all to go back in time, relive the past and experience a day that I am sure we will all remember for years to come."

"Definitely historical," I whispered again.

"Definitely historical." Gabby nodded.

The instant Mrs Peters had finished

telling us her special news, everyone unfolded their arms, forgot to sit up straight and started chatting to each other really excitedly. Going to Bobbington Hall was the best news we had had ALL WEEK! No one had ever heard of Bobbington Hall or knew where Bobbington Hall was, but we knew it wasn't in school. That's the best thing about going on a school trip – you get a whole day off lessons, plus you get to go on an actual coach with actual comfy seats and everything! Going to Bobbington Hall wasn't just special news – it was super-exciting news!

Trouble is, before we could get super excited, Mrs Peters clapped her hands again and told us to get on with our work. She said that at the end of the day she would be giving us a letter about the school trip to take home to our parents, but until the 19th of June came along, it would be lessons as normal. (That's the **trouble with getting super excited.** You're not allowed to do it in class.)

As soon as the bell for morning

break went, everyone ran outside and got super excited in the playground instead.

"Bagsy the seats at the back of the coach," said Jack Beechwhistle before we'd even got as far as the climbing frames.

"Me and Gabby have already bagsied them," I fibbed.

"WHEN?" asked Jack.

"In the corridor straight after lessons," I told him. "Before you, Colin and Harry had even thought of doing any bagsies."

"First one to the hopscotch square wins!" said Jack, racing away.

Whenever something super exciting happens in our school, everyone in my class always heads straight for the hopscotch square. It's like our special super-exciting meeting place. Even Barry Morely goes to the hopscotch square when something super exciting is happening. Barry Morely is the cleverest person in our class. In fact, he's so clever he can do sums in his head. At break times he always sits on the quiet bench, so if he's in the hopscotch square, you can bet something super exciting must be going on!

"What do you think Bobbington Hall will be like?" asked Vicky Carrow.

"Olden," I told her.

"How olden?" asked Jasmine Smart.

"Really olden," I told her.

"I hope it's got a dungeon," said Daniel McNicholl.

12

"Only castles have dungeons," said Barry.

"I hope it's got a moat," said Sanjay Lapore.

"Only castles have moats," said Barry.

"I hope it's got a drawbridge," said Stephanie Brakespeare.

13

"Only castles have drawbridges," said Barry.

I told you Barry Morely was clever.

 "Even if it isn't a castle, it might still have suits of armour in it," said Liam Chaldecott.

"I went to a restaurant once and it had a suit of armour in it!" said Gabby.

"Was it an olden restaurant?" I asked.

"I don't think so," she said. "It had hand driers in the loo and it had an ice-cream factory."

"That's not olden," I told her. "That's newden."

"In the olden days, everyone used to wear suits of armour," said Liam. "I bet Bobbington Hall *has* got suits of armour in it. It might even have choppers and swords to go with them."

"I hope Bobbington Hall has got cannon balls," said Sanjay Lapore.

"I'll tell you what Bobbington Hall will definitely, definitely have," said Jack Beechwhistle, pushing his way through to the very middle of the hopscotch square and putting both hands on his hips.

"WHAT???!" everyone asked at the same time.

"Secret passages," he smiled.

CHAPTER 3

According to Jack Beechwhistle, every olden place has at least one secret passage. Some have about ten. It depends how big and how olden the place is.

"If Bobbington Hall is massive, it will have at least ten secret passages," said Jack. "The secret is finding them."

"What are secret passages for?" asked Melanie Simpson.

"Keeping secrets in," said Jack.

"Olden secrets," I added.

"In olden times there were loads of things that needed keeping secret," said Jack. "There could be olden treasure, there could be olden weapons, there could be olden treasure maps, or even a stash of olden bananas."

"Why would there be a stash of

olden bananas?" asked Liam.

"Because," said Jack, "olden times are when bananas were first invented."

"Not invented," said Barry Morely. "Discovered."

"Same thing," said Jack. "It was around the time of King Henry the Eighth."

"King Charles the First, actually," said Barry.

"Same thing," said Jack. "It was in the really olden days that people got a taste for bananas. Trouble is, because bananas were so expensive, you couldn't just keep them in a fruit bowl. You had to keep them somewhere secret, like a secret passage or a secret hidey-hole – otherwise people might steal them."

"Why were they so expensive?" asked Paula Potts.

"Because they were so rare," said Jack. "In the really olden days, bananas had to be brought all the way to England in ships with no engines. In olden times, engines weren't even invented OR discovered. All olden ships had to make them go was sails, which means they were really slow, because sails are nowhere near as fast as engines, which meant it took months and months for the bananas to arrive."

"Which meant that, when they did arrive in England, they were black," said Barry Morely.

"Yellow," said Jack.

"Black," said Barry.

"Bananas are yellow," said Jack.

"Not when they're months old, they're not," said Barry. "When they're months old, they turn black."

"Same thing," said Jack. "If word got round in olden days that you owned a load of bananas, then every burglar for a hundred miles would come round to your house and try to steal them, whether they were yellow OR black. That's why olden rich people hid their bananas in secret passages."

"Did olden poor people have secret passages too?" I asked.

"There was no point," said Jack, "because olden poor people didn't own anything worth hiding."

"What if you were an olden poor person and one day you were walking along the road and a banana lorry went past, hit a bump and a big bunch of bananas fell off right in front of you, which meant you suddenly got a load of bananas for free?" I asked. "What would you do with them then?"

"You'd either have to eat the whole bunch really fast," said Jack, "or dig a hole in your lawn. You definitely wouldn't have a secret passage to hide them in."

"Lorries didn't exist in the seventeenth century," said Barry Morely. "In the time of Charles the First, everything was transported by horse and cart."

"Same thing," said Jack.

"I'd hardly say a lorry was the same thing as a horse and cart." Barry frowned.

"It was in olden times," said Jack. "Wasn't it, Colin? Wasn't it, Harry?"

"Definitely." They nodded.

That's the **trouble with Colin and Harry**.

They are always on the same side as Jack. I think that's why Barry went back to the quiet bench.

CHAPTER 4

The more everyone thought about secret passages, the more excited we became.

"How can you get into a secret passage?" asked David Alexander.

"Secret ways only," said Jack. "Secret passages never have normal door handles. That would be far too easy for everyone to see. To get into a secret passage, you might have to press a secret button or pull a secret lever or even say some magic words."

"Like 'Open Sesame!'" said Lottie Taylor.

"More magic than that," said Jack.

"What kind of treasure would you find in a secret passage?" asked Melanie Simpson.

"Olden treasure," I told her.

"Coins mostly," said Jack. "Silver coins, gold coins, especially Spanish doubloons."

"Spanish what?" frowned Gabby.

"It's pirate money," said Jack. "Spanish doubloons are great big shiny gold coins made in Spain. Pirate treasure chests are full of them."

"What about English doubloons?" asked Dottie Taylor.

"What about Scottish doubloons?" asked Lottie Taylor.

"There's no such thing as other doubloons," said Jack. "The only doubloons you get are Spanish ones. Plus doubloons aren't the only treasure you find in a secret passage. There might be gold rings, pearl necklaces, diamond bracelets, emerald earrings, rubies, sapphires, even crowns and tiaras."

"All stolen by pirates?" asked Colin.

"Mostly," said Jack.

The more Jack told us about secret passages and secret treasure, the more everyone realized how amazing it would be to find a secret passage at Bobbington Hall. Maybe even ten secret passages!

"What do you think a secret passage looks like inside?" asked Daniel Carrington.

"Really olden," I said.

"Really dark at first," said Jack, "until your eyes get used to it. Once your eyes get used to the dark, I reckon it would be really shadowy and exciting."

"How shadowy?" asked Gabby.

"Yes, how shadowy?" I said.

(Gabby and me don't really like shadows. Especially at bedtime.)

"WELL shadowy," said Harry.

"WELL WELL shadowy," agreed Colin. "Unless you've got a torch."

"I've got a torch!" I said. "I've got a three-colour torch that does red, white and green!"

"White would probably be best in a secret passage," said Jack. "If you step into somewhere that is well well secret and well well dark, then the brighter the torch beam the better. You should definitely take your torch to Bobbington Hall. In fact, we should all take our torches to Bobbington Hall."

"Without Mrs Peters knowing," I said.

"DEFINITELY without Mrs Peters knowing," said Jack. "You can imagine what Mrs Peters would do if she knew we were looking for secret passages on a school trip!"

"You can imagine what Mrs Peters would do if we FOUND a secret passage on a school trip!" said Fiona Tucker. "If we find a secret  passage at Bobbington Hall, we will all be rich!"

"Especially if it's full of pirate treasure," said Colin.

"Mrs Peters would be so jealous if we found a load of pirate treasure on our school trip," said Gabby.

"I bet she'd confiscate it!"

"I bet she'd keep it in the drawer of her desk."

"There's no way she'd let us have any of the treasure," said Nishta Bagwhat. "Especially if it was diamonds and rubies and emeralds and sapphires."

"Double especially if it was doublyoons!" laughed Gabby.

"The only thing she would let us keep is the mouldy bananas," I said.

"That's decided then," said Jack. "If we look for secret passages at Bobbington Hall, then we'll have to do it secretly. Which means we're going to have to do a secret pact! Agreed?"

"AGREED!" everyone shouted.

CHAPTER 5

The **trouble with secret pacts** is they are really hard to keep secret when there are thirty of you.

Especially if there are teachers nearby who might be watching or listening to what you're saying. Luckily, I had a brilliant idea.

"Everyone put their arms around each other and form a circle," I said, "so it looks like we're going to play American football."

"Are we actually going to play American football?" asked Paula Potts, putting her arm round Gabby and then bending down.

"Of course not," I whispered. "No one knows how to play American football. We just don't want to look suspicious."

Once we had formed our secret circle, saying the secret pact was easy.

Well, it was once Vicky Carrow had decided what part of the circle she was going to join.

"Repeat after me," whispered Jack. "We swear . . ."

"WE SWEAR . . ."

"That by the power of this secret pact . . ."

"THAT BY THE POWER OF THIS SECRET PACT . . ."

"We will look and look and look for secret passages . . ."

"WE WILL LOOK AND LOOK AND LOOK FOR SECRET PASSAGES . . ."

"At Bobbington Hall . . ."

"AT BOBBINGTON HALL . . ."

"Without Mrs Peters ever knowing . . ."

"WITHOUT MRS PETERS EVER KNOWING . . ."

"And if anyone blabs . . ."

"AND IF ANYONE BLABS . . ."

"Or gives the game away . . ."

"OR GIVES THE GAME AWAY . . ."

"Their tongue will drop off . . ."

"THEIR TONGUE WILL DROP OFF . . ."

"And so will their head . . ."

"AND SO WILL THEIR HEAD . . ."

"Amen."

"AMEN."

When we got back to our classroom after morning break, Mrs Peters had no idea that we'd made a secret pact. As far as Mrs

Peters was concerned, it was lessons as usual. But it wasn't. Because for the rest of the day, everyone in my class hardly thought about lessons at all. All we thought about was secret passages.

In secret!

CHAPTER 6

When I looked around me during afternoon lessons, I could tell that absolutely everyone was thinking about secret passages. Apart from Barry Morely.

Stephanie Brakespeare was staring at the wall, Liam Chaldecott was looking under his desk, Paula Potts was turning the handles on the stationery cupboard and Nishta Bagwhat was trying to move the wastepaper bin with her toe. Everyone was looking for secret passages!

But only when Mrs Peters wasn't looking. If you've made a secret pact and you don't want your teacher to know, you have to be SO, SO CAREFUL!

"Do you think there are any secret passages at home?" whispered Gabby when Mrs Peters was wiping the whiteboard.

"I don't know," I whispered back. "I've never really looked for any."

"Do you think, if we found some Spanish doubloons and took them to the bank, they'd swap them for proper English money?" whispered Gabby when Mrs Peters was refilling her stapler.

"I reckon so," I whispered. "Spanish doubloons are some of the most valuable things on Earth. Especially if they're nice and shiny."

"If the bank gave us loads of proper money for our doubloons, we could share it," Gabby whispered.

"And spend it," I whispered back.

"I'd buy a pony," whispered Gabby.

"I'd buy a monkey," I whispered back.

"I'd buy a Go-Pro," whispered Gabby.

"I'd buy a go-rilla!" I giggled, without meaning to. But it was too late.

The **trouble with giggles** is they are a bit louder than whispers. Especially if you giggle through your nose.

"DAISY! GABRIELLA! If you have something to say, then perhaps you'd like to say it to the whole class," said Mrs Peters, giving us both really frowny looks. "DO you have something you'd like to share with the class?"

"No, Mrs Peters," I said.

"No, Mrs Peters," said Gabby.

"Then less whispering and more long division from the two of you please," she said.

"As soon as we get home tonight, let's look for secret passages," whispered Gabby in the whisperiest whisper she could do.

"Good idea," I wrote on the back of my maths book in the quietest writing I could write!

When the bell went at the end of the day, Gabby and I couldn't wait to get to the school gates to tell my mum all about Bobbington Hall.

We didn't tell her about our secret pact though, in case she blabbed to Mrs Peters or one of the other mums.

Mum said she was sure the trip would be an educational day for both of us. But me and Gabby knew it would be much better than that. A day off school looking for secret passages was going to be absolutely awesome! Almost as awesome as finding an actual secret passage in our own actual home! Especially a secret passage with actual treasure in it.

As soon as I got home, I raced

straight upstairs, changed out of my uniform and started hunting for secret passages right away. Starting with my wardrobe.

The **trouble with my wardrobe** is it definitely looks like it could have a secret passage in it.

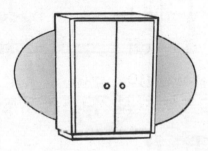

Trouble is, when I opened the door and peeped inside, there was only enough space for clothes and hangers.

Even after I'd completely emptied my wardrobe and climbed right inside, I couldn't find a secret passage, or even a secret door.

Luckily, Jack had warned everyone just how hard it was to find a secret passage, so there was no way I was going to give up.

I looked under my bed.

I looked in my sock drawer.

I looked in my
knicker drawer.

I looked in
my toy box.

I even looked
down the
sleeves of my
pyjamas.

When I'd finished looking in my bedroom, I totally kept on looking. I looked in my mum's bedroom. I looked in the lounge. I looked in the kitchen. I looked in the shed. In fact, I only stopped looking when my mum found me trying to unscrew the bathroom cabinet to see behind.

When I phoned Gabby to tell her I hadn't found any secret passages anywhere, she said she hadn't either.

"The only place I haven't looked," she said, "is down the loo."

"Down the loo!?" I said. "You couldn't squeeze down the loo!"

"Alice in Wonderland could," said Gabby. "If she could squeeze down a rabbit hole, she could definitely squeeze down the loo."

"If you squeezed down the loo, I don't think you'd end up in Wonderland," I said. "I think you'd end up in Poopyland."

"That's why I haven't tried it," said Gabby.

"Maybe our houses aren't old enough to have secret passages," I said. "Maybe the only place we'll ever find a secret passage is Bobbington Hall."

"You're probably right," said Gabby. "Let's keep looking though. We've still got twelve more sleeps to go!"

CHAPTER 7

Eleven sleeps later, me and Gabby still hadn't found a secret passage. Neither had anyone in my class, even though absolutely everyone had been looking.

Vicky Carrow had found the lid to her mum and dad's water meter, Lottie and Dottie had bent a screwdriver trying to lift up a man-hole cover in their back garden, Nishta had got stung by stinging nettles uncovering the secret door to a cucumber frame, Colin had discovered two different ways into his grandma's coal bunker (but only found coal inside it), and Paula Potts had accidentally pulled the handle off her mum and dad's drinks cabinet after saying the wrong magic words.

No one, absolutely no one, in my class had found an actual secret passage. Including Jack Beechwhistle!

Jack said that just because we hadn't found a secret passage in our homes, it didn't mean there weren't any.

"The reason secret passages are called secret," he said, "is because they are totally camouflaged into the room. Sometimes the only way you will ever find them is with a bit of secret luck."

"What kind of secret luck?" I asked.

"The kind of secret luck I saw in a TV film once," said Jack.

"Was the TV film really olden?" I asked.

"Older than that," said Jack. "It was in black and white."

"Black and white!" everyone gasped. "How could anyone watch a film in black and white?"

"I'd watch a film in sky-blue pink if it was exciting," said Jack. "When a film is in black and white, all you have to do is imagine the missing colours."

"Did the film have a secret passage in it?" asked Gabby.

"Sure did," said Jack. "AND it showed you the secret way to get inside!"

As soon as we realized that Jack had seen an actual secret passage in an actual film, plus the actual film had showed you the actual way to get inside the actual secret passage, we begged him to tell us more. Even if he told us in black and white!

So he did!

"Imagine the creepiest, oldest, cobwebbiest house in the world," Jack said.

"WE'RE IMAGINING! WE'RE IMAGINING!" I told him.

"Now imagine a really nervous man sitting at the table in the dining room, being served his dinner by a really creepy butler . . ." Jack shivered.

"The butler walks up to the table, bows, puts down the dinner, bows again and then leaves the room."

"I bet the dinner has got poison in it," said Sanjay Lapore.

"I bet it's got peas in it." I shuddered.

"It hasn't got anything dangerous in it," said Jack. "It's just a normal dinner, BUT . . ."

"BUT WHAT?" we asked.

"But," said Jack, "after just one taste the really nervous man decides it needs some extra salt and pepper and . . ."

"AND WHAT?" we asked.

"And reaches out really nervously," said Jack.

"AND?" we asked.

"And," said Jack, "because he's really nervous, picks up a candlestick instead!"

"BY MISTAKE?" we asked.

"By mistake," said Jack.

"AND???" we asked.

"And as soon as he lifts up the candlestick, a secret passage opens up right in front of his eyes!"

"WHERE?" we gasped.

"In the dining room!" said Jack.

"BUT WHERE EXACTLY?" we gasped.

"In the wall in front of him," said Jack. "Without any warning, a big piece of wooden panelling just slides back magically and reveals a secret passage behind!!"

"AND ALL BECAUSE HE PICKED UP A CANDLESTICK BY MISTAKE!" I gasped.

"Not just any old candlestick," said Jack. "A secret candlestick attached to a secret string that was threaded through a secret hole in the table, down through another secret hole in the table leg, under the floor of the dining room, and then invisibly all the way across the room and up behind the secret panelling to a secret switch that made the secret wooden door open automatically!"

"THAT'S AMAZING!" gasped Sanjay.
"THAT'S INCREDIBLE!" gulped Nishta.

"That's SECRET LUCK!" Jack smiled. "With a bit of secret luck, one of us is bound to find a secret passage at Bobbington Hall."

"Especially if it's got secret candlesticks!" said Gabby, clapping her hands.

"DOUBLE ESPECIALLY if it has secret candlesticks." Jack grinned.

CHAPTER 8

By the time we'd got to the day before the school trip, my class knew so much about secret candlesticks, secret treasure, secret buttons, secret levers, secret passages and secret luck, we were almost exploding with excitement. At last, at last, at last, after two weeks of waiting, there was only one more sleep to go!

Even Mrs Peters seemed excited!

Except she wasn't. She had another important announcement to make. Two actually . . .

"Children," she said, "I would like to introduce you to Miss Fletcher. Miss Fletcher is a teaching assistant and will be accompanying us on our trip to Bobbington Hall tomorrow."

"I wondered who she was," whispered Gabby.

"Me too," I whispered back.

"Now then," said Mrs Peters, folding her arms. "The weather is set fair and our visit promises to be a treat for us all . . ."

The instant Mrs Peters said "treat for us all", everyone in my class wanted to unfold their arms, stop sitting up straight and get even more excited than we had nearly two weeks ago, but we didn't. We stayed sitting up straight and kept folding our arms instead. Because Mrs Peters' eyeballs said we had to. So did Miss Fletcher's.

And we were right too!

"Before we go to Bobbington Hall tomorrow, children," said Mrs Peters, "I want you to take a moment to look around you. I want you to look at yourselves, look at your classmates, look long and hard, think long and hard, and tell me what you see."

"CLASS 4C!" shouted Paula Potts, trying to win a house point.

"An alien," said Jack Beechwhistle, pointing straight at me.

"I'll tell you what we see, Jack." Mrs Peters frowned. "What we see is an entire class on their very best behaviour."

"Apart from Jack Beechwhistle," I said, poking my tongue out at him in revenge.

"Apart from Jack Beechwhistle," agreed Mrs Peters. "What everyone will see – when Jack has quite finished pulling alien faces – is an entire class being not just school-children, but 'school ambassadors' . . . 'SCHOOL AMBASSADORS'," Mrs Peters said again, writing *School Ambassadors* on the whiteboard and then giving the Ambassadors bit a double underline.

"Now then, children, for five house points, can anyone tell the class what a school ambassador is?"

The **trouble with five house points** is everyone wants to win five house points. Only no one knew the answer to the question.

Apart from Barry Morely.

"A school ambassador is someone who represents the school in the very best way," he said. "They wear their school uniform with pride, they are really well behaved, they don't get into trouble and they make people who see us think our school is the best."

And guess what? He was right. Well, Mrs Peters said he was.

So did my mum when I met her at the school gates.

When I told my mum that I was going to be an ambassador for the school, she went really quiet. I think she was so proud she couldn't speak.

As soon as we got home, I asked her to make my packed lunch straight away, in case she forgot in the morning.

"Would you like a banana in your lunch box?" she asked.

"Yes, three, please," I said, "and four chocolate biscuits, nine bags of crisps, a really big bottle of lemonade, some cheese strings, eight yoghurts, eleven scotch eggs, a packet of crunchy creams, a box of strawberry Dip Dabs and some emergency bubble gum."

Well, it was worth a try.

CHAPTER 9

When I woke up this morning, it only took me about two blinks to remember that it was the actual day of the actual school trip. About one and a half blinks actually.

No, one and a bit.

Maybe even less.

Anyway, I absolutely couldn't wait to put my school uniform on. Trouble is, my mum was still ironing it.

"HURRY UP!" I told her when I ran into the kitchen. "I'm supposed to be being a school ambassador!"

The **trouble with being a school ambassador** is you need to wear your school uniform. Because school ambassadors don't wear pyjamas.

"You'll look a lot more like an ambassador without the creases," said Mum, holding up my cardigan and giving it a funny look. "I don't know what you get up to all day at school, but your uniform looks like it's been jumped on by an elephant."

"I'd be dead if I'd been jumped on by an elephant," I told her. "And anyway, we're not allowed elephants at school."

"A rhinoceros then," said my mum, moving on to my school dress.

As soon as all the creases in my uniform had been ironed out, I raced back up to my bedroom and got dressed.

By the time I had eaten breakfast, checked the batteries in my torch and polished my lunch box, we were ready to go!

You should have seen how sunny it was when we left for school. It was an absolutely perfect day for a school trip!

When I rang Gabby's doorbell, I was absolutely sure she wouldn't be in the slightest bit creased either. And I was right. Her cardigan, her skirt, her socks, her blouse and even her shoes looked absolutely brand new. Mostly because they were all brand new, but I'm sure her mum must have had to iron them a bit. Not including her shoes.

"Aren't school trips exciting!" said Gabby, springing out of her house, grabbing my hand and then bouncing us both all the way down her front path to where my mum was waiting.

"I got my mum to make me cheese sandwiches!" Gabby said.

"ME TOO!" I said. "THAT MEANS WE'RE MATCHING!"

As soon as I realized that Gabby and I had matching sandwiches, I just knew our trip to Bobbington Hall was going to be the best ever. When we reached the hopscotch square, I was one hundred percent definitely totally certain!!!

You should have seen how smart everyone in my class looked!

They had all polished their shoes and made them look really shiny. Paula Potts had had her jumper washed.

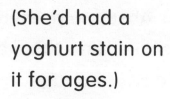
(She'd had a yoghurt stain on it for ages.)

Nishta had a new school blouse

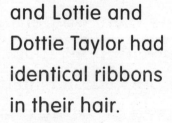
and Lottie and Dottie Taylor had identical ribbons in their hair.

Liam Chaldecott even had a side parting!

Absolutely everyone in my class looked like school ambassadors. Well, nearly everyone.

The only person who still had creases on him was Jack Beechwhistle, because his mum had woken up with a headache. And an arm ache. And a hand ache. So she couldn't pick up her iron.

Which was a bit of a shame for Jack. And his mum.

Jack didn't mind though. All he cared about was getting on the coach!

All EVERYONE cared about was GETTING ON THE COACH!

CHAPTER 10

The **trouble with getting on coaches** is you can't just get on them.

As soon as Mrs Peters told us that the coach had arrived outside our school, Gabby and I wanted to race out of the classroom, sprint down the corridor, shoot across the playground and get right to the front of the queue.

If you get right to the front of the queue, you can get right to the back of the coach. FIRST!

Trouble is, Mrs Peters wouldn't let us. Neither would Miss Fletcher. Instead, we had to stand up like ambassadors, put our chairs under our tables like ambassadors, form a line like ambassadors, and walk down the corridor and across the playground like ambassadors. We even had to fold our arms like ambassadors before the coach driver would open the door!

If we hadn't had to do everything like ambassadors, Gabby and me would have been the first ones on the coach for sure.

But we weren't, because Jack, Harry and Colin got ahead of us.

The **trouble with Jack, Harry and Colin getting ahead of us** is they cheated.

Because they didn't put their chairs under the tables like ambassadors at all.

And WE DID.

PLUS when everyone was told to

walk like ambassadors, they did whopping great strides to get to the front instead.

And WE didn't.

And they did whopping great strides all the way down the corridor.

And across the playground.

And all the way to the coach.

Which, if you're being a school ambassador, is illegal.

But Mrs Peters and Miss Fletcher were too busy to notice.

So they got away with it.

Well, they thought they'd got away with it.

Just before the coach driver opened the door to let everybody on, Gabby and me marched right up to the front of the line and reminded Jack, Colin and Harry that we had bagsied the seats at the back.

But they didn't listen.

They pretended to listen. They even nodded their heads at us and everything. But guess what? When me and Gabby finally got all the way from the middle of the line to the back of the coach, guess who was sitting on the seats we had bagsied?

Jack Beechwhistle, Harry Bayliss and Colin Kettle, that's who.

"We bagsied those seats!" I said, putting my school bag on the luggage rack and giving all three of them one of my evillest stares. "In fact, we bagsied all five of those seats!"

"Tough," said Jack, turning sideways and putting his feet on the two spaces left.

The **trouble with someone turning sideways and putting their feet on the two spaces left** is that it makes you want to sit on the back seat even more.

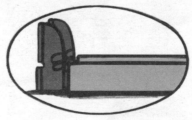

So we did.

Without telling Jack we were going to.

"You're breaking my legs!" he said, feeling the full weight of our girl power on his leg bones.

"Move them then!" I told him. "Share the seat or you'll never walk again!"

"I can't move them, you're crushing me!" he exaggerated. "I'm suffocating!" he fibbed. "I can't breathe! I can't feel my toes. I can't feel my ankles. I can't feel my knees!"

I can promise you, Jack Beechwhistle won't be sitting sideways on any more coach seats after that!

CHAPTER 11

Once we'd forced Jack to share the back seats with us, we all started thinking about secret passages again. Not just secret passages either!

"Have I told you about paintings with moving eyeballs?" whispered Jack as we waved goodbye to our school.

"No!" Gabby and I gasped.

"TELL US NOW!"

If Jack hadn't started telling me and Gabby about paintings with moving eyeballs, I reckon the journey to Bobbington Hall might have gone quite slowly. But paintings with moving eyeballs are one of the most exciting things on earth. Well, almost as exciting as secret passages!

Especially when Jack does his creepy voice.

"Imagine the creepiest, oldest, cobwebbiest house in the world," he whispered.

"Like the one in that film you told us about?" we whispered back.

"Exactly like the one in that film,

only times it by a thousand." Jack nodded.

"A thousand?" gasped Gabby.

"A thousand," repeated Jack. "At least."

"That IS creepy," I said.

"That IS cobwebby," said Gabby.

"Now imagine," said Jack, "that you are all alone in that house. Alone in a room with a creepy, cobwebby painting of a person on the wall."

"Which wall?" asked Gabby.

"It doesn't matter which wall," said Jack. "All that matters is that, although you are TOTALLY alone in the room, you have the creepiest, cobwebbiest feeling that you are being watched."

"I'm imagining. I'm imagining!" I nodded.

"Watched by who?" asked Gabby.

"You don't know," said Jack. "You can't see them. All you know is that they can see you."

"Paintings of people can't look at you," I said. "They're made of paint!"

"They can if the eyeballs on the painting have been cut out and someone is looking through the holes," said Jack.

"Who is looking through?!" I asked.

"The person hiding in the secret passage directly behind the painting," said Jack.

"So you mean secret passages have secret eyeholes too!" I gasped.

"Eyeholes, spyholes, it doesn't matter what you call them, but yes, sometimes in really old places with really old people paintings, they totally do."

"Will there be people paintings on the wall at Bobbington Hall?"

"Bound to be," said Jack.

"And will they have moving eyeballs?"

"Perhaps," said Jack. "It's really hard to tell."

"How can we tell if the people paintings on the wall at Bobbington

Hall have moving eyeballs?" I asked.

"The only way is to turn your head quickly enough to see the eyeballs move," Jack said.

"Like this," said Gabby, looking out of the coach window and then darting her head back towards us.

"Times that by a thousand too," said Jack.

"That's fast," said Gabby.

"That's supersonic," I said.

"Well, that's what you need to be," whispered Jack. "If you want to see the moving eyeballs in a people painting, you need to be able to turn your head supersonically fast."

As soon as we realized that Bobbington Hall might not only have secret passages but secret eyeballs too, we started practising our supersonic head turns straight away.

"You pretend you're all alone in the house," I told Gabby, "and I'll pretend I'm a painting with moving eyeballs. If you turn your head fast enough and see my eyeballs moving, then you win. If you don't see my moving eyeballs, I win."

"Like this?" said Gabby, looking out of the coach window, then turning her head round as fast as she could.

"No, like this," said Jack, not seeing

my moving eyeballs either.

"No, like this," said Colin, not even getting close.

"LIKE THIS!" said Harry, turning his head too quickly and pulling one of the muscles in his neck.

"Let me try," I said, giving Gabby a turn to be the moving eyeballs.

"SAW THEM!" I cheered, looking away when Gabby wasn't expecting it and then turning my head back super-duper-sonically fast.

"I haven't even started moving my eyeballs yet!" protested Gabby.

"Well, I definitely saw them move," I told her.

"Let *me* be the moving eyeballs," said Jack.

"Let *me* be the moving eyeballs," said Colin, then Harry.

Honestly, I think we would have played "moving eyeballs" all the way to Bobbington Hall if Mrs Peters hadn't suddenly stood up at the front of the coach and started clapping her hands.

"Children," she said, "we will be arriving at Bobbington Hall very shortly. But before we do so, can I please have your fullest and most ambassadorial attention?"

That's the **trouble with teachers**. They always stop you when you're having fun.

CHAPTER 12

"Behold, my young ambassadors," said Mrs Peters, holding something up for everyone to see. "THE AMBASSADOR'S GOLDEN CUSHION!"

The **trouble** **with** **the** **AMBASSADOR'S GOLDEN CUSHION** is that no one in my class had ever seen an Ambassador's Golden Cushion before. Especially a golden cushion with dangly golden tassels!

"Sit back down in your seats please, children," said Mrs Peters when she realized we were all getting super excited again. "Sit back down in your seats and listen to what Miss Fletcher has to say very carefully."

As soon as everyone had sat back down in their seats, Miss Fletcher got up out of hers.

"The winner of this lovely comfy cushion," she said, taking it from Mrs Peters and stroking it with the back of her hand, "the lucky winner of the Ambassador's Golden Cushion will be allowed to sit on it in class for ONE WHOLE WEEK!"

"ONE WHOLE WEEK?!!!!" everyone gasped.

"I'd love to sit on a golden cushion in class," said Gabby.

"I'd love to sit on a golden cushion in class too," said Harry.

EVERYONE absolutely loved the idea of sitting on a golden cushion in class!

Trouble is, when we heard what Mrs Peters said next, we went off golden cushions completely.

"The lucky winner of the Ambassador's Golden Cushion," she said, clapping her hands really loudly and making us all sit down again, "will be the clever ambassador who answers the most questions on their Bobbington Hall worksheet correctly."

"Bobbington Hall WHAT sheet?" gasped Jack.

"Worksheet," groaned Harry.

"Worksheet?" groaned Colin.

"Worksheet," groaned absolutely everyone on the coach.

Apart from Barry Morely.

"We haven't come to Bobbington

Hall to do worksheets!" whispered Jack. "We've come to look for secret passages!"

"And people paintings with moving eyeballs," I whispered back.

"And secret treasure," whispered Gabby.

"Spanish doubloons are far more golden than golden cushions," whispered Jack.

"So are Spanish golden swords," said Harry.

"And Spanish golden necklaces," I whispered.

"I haven't come to Bobbington Hall to sit on a golden cushion," said Jack.

"I've come here to look for golden treasure!"

"EVERYONE HAS!" I nodded.

Mrs Peters hadn't though. Neither had Miss Fletcher. They had brought us to Bobbington Hall to do work.

"Your worksheets have been specially written by the owners of Bobbington Hall and will be given to you on our arrival," Miss Fletcher said. "Please remember to take your school bags and your packed lunches with you when you leave the coach, and take your pens and pencils with you too."

"PENS AND PENCILS?" I gasped.

"I've only brought a lunch box and a torch!" whispered Colin.

"So have I," gulped Harry.

So had everyone on the coach.

Apart from Barry Morely.

"How are we meant to fill in a worksheet if we haven't got any pens or pencils?" asked Gabby.

"How are we meant to look for

secret passages if we're filling in a worksheet?" asked Jack.

"We need to make a new secret pact," I whispered, "and we need to make one fast!"

The **trouble with making a new secret pact fast** is you can't do it on a school coach, because the space down the middle is too small to make a secret circle.

Luckily, just as we were pulling into the car park, I had a genius idea.

"As soon as we arrive at actual Bobbington Hall, we must tell Mrs Peters that we need to go to the loo!" I whispered.

"But I don't need to go to the loo," said Gabby. "I went before I left home."

"It doesn't matter," I said. "That's what we must do. Now, Harry, tap Sanjay on the shoulder. Gabby, you tap Liberty on the shoulder. Tell them the secret plan and get them to pass it on!"

By the time the coach driver had switched off his engine, everyone sitting on both sides of the coach knew exactly what we were going to do.

Not including Mrs Peters. Or Miss Fletcher. No one said a word to Mrs Peters until we were standing outside the actual front door of actual Bobbington Hall.

CHAPTER 13

You should have seen how olden the outside of Bobbington Hall was! The walls were made of olden bricks. The windows were made of olden glass. The roof was all olden and slopey. The chimneys were all olden and twisty. The front door was really olden. The front step was really olden. Even the man standing on the step was really olden.

"Good morning, children," he said. "Welcome to Bobbington Hall, the home of the Frostwycke family for five centuries, right up to the present day. My name is Mr Rowley and I will be your guide for—"

"EXCUSE ME, MRS PETERS!" I said, putting up my hand. "I need to go to the loo."

"EXCUSE ME, MRS PETERS, WE NEED TO GO TO THE LOO TOO!" said absolutely everyone in my class at exactly the same time.

Including Barry Morely!

As soon as absolutely everyone told Mrs Peters that they needed to go to the loo at exactly the same time, Mrs Peters started to look quite olden too.

"Really?" she sighed.

"REALLY." We nodded.

"I am so sorry, Mr Rowley," Mrs Peters said. "Please could you direct the children to your toilet facilities?"

"Of course," said Mr Rowley. "Please follow me inside."

You should have seen how olden it was inside Bobbington Hall!!

"There's going to be secret passages everywhere," whispered Jack.

"And moving eyeballs," I whispered back. "Look! Three people paintings in a row!"

Honestly, I'd never seen an inside so olden. The floor was made of olden stones and the walls were made of olden wood. The tables had olden tablecloths on them, plus the chairs had olden cushions (but not golden ones). Bobbington Hall was completely olden, absolutely everywhere we looked!!!

Including the toilets!

When me and Gabby opened the door to the girls' toilet, we couldn't believe our eyes.

Both sinks had an olden bar of soap!

Both plugs were attached to olden chains!

The olden hand drier only did paper towels!

Plus, if you wanted to flush an olden toilet, you had to pull an olden chain!

Not that any-one actually went to the toilet. We were far too busy forming our secret circle.

"Are you ready?" I whispered, tightening my grip around Gabby's shoulder and concentrating on getting the words of our new secret pact exactly right.

"READY," everyone whispered.

"Then repeat after me . . ." I said.

132

"We swear . . ."

"WE SWEAR . . ."

"That by the power of this new secret pact . . ."

"THAT BY THE POWER OF THIS NEW SECRET PACT . . ."

"That the boys are doing as well . . ."

"THAT THE BOYS ARE DOING AS WELL . . ."

"At the same time in the other toilet . . ."

"AT THE SAME TIME IN THE OTHER TOILET . . ."

(I added that bit myself.)

"We swear that we will look and look and look for secret passages . . ."

"WE SWEAR THAT WE WILL LOOK AND LOOK AND LOOK FOR SECRET PASSAGES . . ."

"And secret treasure . . ."

"AND SECRET TREASURE . . ."

"And secret luck . . ."

"AND SECRET LUCK . . ."

"At Bobbington Hall . . ."

"AT BOBBINGTON HALL . . ."

"At the same time as only pretending to do our worksheets . . ."

"AT THE SAME TIME AS ONLY PRETENDING TO DO OUR WORK-SHEETS . . ."

"But not really doing our work-sheets . . ."

"BUT NOT REALLY DOING OUR WORKSHEETS . . ."

"Because worksheets get in the way of looking for secret passages . . ."

"BECAUSE WORKSHEETS GET IN THE WAY OF LOOKING FOR SECRET PASSAGES . . ."

"And if anyone blabs . . ."

"AND IF ANYONE BLABS . . ."

"Or gives the game away . . ."

"OR GIVES THE GAME AWAY . . ."

"They will turn into mouldy bananas . . ."

"THEY WILL TURN INTO MOULDY BANANAS . . ."

"And be eaten by a mouldy

gorilla . . ."

"AND BE EATEN BY A MOULDY
GORILLA . . ."

"Amen!"

"AMEN!!!!!"

As soon as the boys came out of the boys' toilet, I asked Jack if he had spoken to Barry.

"Yes," he said. "Barry didn't mind saying the secret pact, but he still wants to do the worksheet as well."

"He likes doing worksheets, doesn't he?" I whispered.

"I think so, yes," Jack whispered back.

"Did you ask him what he's got in his pencil case?" I whispered. "If everyone is going to pretend to be filling in worksheets, we're going to need to borrow thirty pencils and thirty pens."

"He's only got two pens and four pencils," he whispered back.

The **trouble with Barry Morely only having two pens and four pencils** is it meant we were twenty-eight pens and twenty-six pencils short. (Gabby did the maths.)

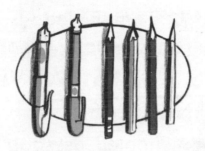

"What's Mrs Peters going to say when she finds out that no one has brought any pens or pencils with them?" whispered Harry.

"Apart from Barry Morely," whispered Gabby.

"She's going to be really cross," whispered Sanjay.

"She's going to go completely loopy-loo," whispered Liam.

"Not if we tell her all at once," I whispered. "If we tell her all at once, she won't know who to tell off first!"

"MRS PETERS, WE'VE LEFT OUR PENCIL CASES AT HOME!" everybody shouted as soon as Mrs Peters arrived with our worksheets.

"REALLY?" she sighed.

"Really," we said.

Apart from Barry Morely.

Thank goodness Bobbington Hall had a gift shop!

And Miss Fletcher had her credit card with her too!!!

CHAPTER 14

As soon as Mrs Peters had given us our new Bobbington Hall pens and pencils, some people in my class even half fancied doing a worksheet. Me almost included – though when I saw how many questions there were, I nearly fainted.

50 questions!!!

Over four pages!!!!

Some of the questions even had an A and a B!

"I knew it," sighed Jack, folding up his worksheet and squeezing it into his back pocket. "There isn't a single question about secret passages."

"Or olden bananas," said Gabby.

"At least we're allowed to guess the answer to question 50," said Dottie Taylor.

"Are we?" said everyone, turning to the very last question on the very last page.

50. Guess how many roof tiles there are on the roof of Bobbington Hall!

"What's a roof tile?" asked Paula Potts.

"It's the bit on the roof that stops the rain getting in," I told her. "Like a brick, only flatter and slopier."

"There must be hundreds of them!" gasped Sanjay.

"There must be millions of them!" gasped Vicky.

"It would take someone about ten weeks to count all the roof tiles on this place!" said Jack, folding his arms and looking really fed up. "We haven't come to Bobbington Hall to count roof tiles. We've come here to look for secret passages!"

"And paintings with moving eyeballs," whispered Gabby.

"The best way to guesstimate the number of roof tiles on a house is to count the number of tiles there are in one row going across, then count the number of rows there are going down, multiply the two numbers together, deduct, say, ten for each chimney, and that should give you a pretty good approximation," said Barry.

"Well, MOST of us have come here to look for secret passages," said Jack.

"I definitely have," I said.

"So have I," said Gabby.

And so had everyone else in my class. ABSOLUTELY EVERYONE had come to Bobbington Hall to look for secret passages!

Apart from Barry Morely.

Barry had answered twelve questions before Mr Rowley had even started his guided tour.

CHAPTER 15

The **trouble with guided tours** is they are nowhere near as exciting as looking for secret passages. Or paintings with moving eyeballs. Unless you're Mrs Peters and Miss Fletcher.

"Daisy and Gabriella, will you please stop looking around like that while Mr Rowley is speaking," said Mrs Peters, before we'd even had a chance to check out the three people paintings on the wall.

"Jack, will you stop tapping on the walls," said Miss Fletcher.

"Nishta, put that candlestick down."

"Lottie, will you stop making the floorboards creak."

"Paula, will you get up off your hands and knees please!"

Honestly, everyone in my class was so keen to be the first person to find a secret passage we almost forgot that Mrs Peters and Miss Fletcher and Mr Rowley were there!

When we went through to the next room, things got even more exciting!

There were more olden candlesticks for us to lift up, more people paintings to check out, two olden doorknobs to twist, six olden vases to look under, a massive olden fireplace with a massive olden chimney to peer up, an olden rug to roll back, plus a proper olden grandfather clock that didn't just tell the time – it had an

olden glass door too!

As soon as everyone saw the olden glass door on the grandfather clock, we knew there could be a secret passage inside.

Luckily for me and Gabby, Vicky Carrow was the first one to open the door and squeeze inside.

The **trouble with opening the door of a grandfather clock and squeezing inside** is there isn't very much room to move.

Especially once you've got both feet in. Double especially if you've still got your school bag on your shoulders.

When Mrs Peters turned round and saw Vicky wedged inside the grandfather clock, she turned white.

"What on earth are you doing, Victoria?!!!!" she said. "Is this the behaviour of a school ambassador? I certainly think it is NOT!"

Mr Rowley didn't think so either, so once Vicky had been unwedged, Mrs Peters sent her back to the coach with Miss Fletcher. For the rest of the day.

"We need to be more secret," I whispered to Gabby. "We need to look for secret passages, but without Mrs Peters or Mr Rowley seeing."

"And we mustn't squeeze into any more grandfather clocks," whispered Gabby.

"DEFINITELY no more squeezing into grandfather clocks," I whispered. "Pass it on."

The **trouble with passing it on** is, the next room we went into was even more exciting!

"Welcome to the Great Hall," said Mr Rowley.

"WOH!" gasped Liam Chaldecott, not very secretly at all. "A SUIT OF ARMOUR! AND LOOK – IT'S GOT A CHOPPER! I told you there would be a suit of armour with a chopper at Bobbington Hall!"

Liam was right. There, before our very eyes, was an actual suit of olden armour holding an actual olden chopper in both olden hands!

As soon as we realized we were in a room with an olden suit of armour in it, we just knew we were **really, really close to finding a secret passage!**

"Try looking under those flags on the wall," whispered Jack.

"Try turning the candlesticks on that table," whispered Harry.

"Try lifting the latch on that window," whispered Colin.

162

There were all sorts of secret things to try in the Great Hall. There were more people paintings to check out.

There was more wooden panelling to tap.

There were table legs to twist . . .

163

drawers to
open . . .

a giant wooden
chest with a
keyhole to peep
through . . .

cushions to
look under . . .

and olden photo-
graphs to turn
upside down.

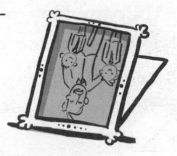

There was even
a dead fox's
nose to press!

Luckily, me and Gabby tried
absolutely everything EXCEPT pulling
the chopper on the suit of armour.

The **trouble with pulling the chopper on a suit of armour** is, the chopper might not actually be the secret lever to a secret passage.

It might just be a chopper.

Attached to a suit of armour.

Which means it will be quite hard to pull.

Unless you get more than one person to pull it.

The **trouble with more than one person pulling the chopper on a suit of olden armour** is it might not just be the chopper that moves. It might be the whole suit of armour.

When the olden suit of armour hit the olden floor, everyone in the room really jumped.

I think Mr Rowley nearly had a heart attack.

Mrs Peters definitely *did* have a heart attack. Well, she definitely had a purply pink fit.

"WHAT THE—? WHO THE—?" she spluttered. "IS THIS A NIGHTMARE THAT I AM ABOUT TO WAKE UP FROM????!!!!"

Trouble is, it wasn't. The olden suit of armour had definitely fallen over, hit the stone floor and kind of fallen apart. Not only that – the chopper had nearly chopped off Nishta Bagwhat's legs at the ankles.

Thank goodness she had jumped up at just the right time or she would never have played hopscotch again.

"LIAM CHALDECOTT AND DANIEL MCNICHOLL...IF YOU THINK THIS IS THE WAY TO WIN THE AMBASSADOR'S GOLDEN CUSHION, THEN I PROMISE THAT YOU ARE VERY MUCH MISTAKEN!" shouted Mrs Peters. "GO AND JOIN VICTORIA AND MISS FLETCHER ON THE COACH THIS INSTANT!"

So they did.
Because they had no choice.

Because Mrs Peters was turning even pinkier and purplier.

Which meant that our class only had twenty-seven ambassadors left.

"At least we've got more chance of winning the golden cushion," whispered Gabby as some other Bobbington Hall people came into the room and took the armour away in a wheelbarrow.

"Yes, but we've got less chance of finding a secret passage!" I whispered. "The more people we've got looking for secret passages, the more things we can do to try to get some secret luck."

"Not including pulling choppers," whispered Gabby.

"DEFINITELY NOT including pulling choppers," I agreed.

CHAPTER 16

By the time Mr Rowley had guided us through three more olden rooms, five more school ambassadors had been sent back to the coach.

Sanjay Lapore got sent back to the coach for pulling a knob off the stairs.

Chelsea Brent got sent back to the coach for forgetting that the vase she

turned upside down had a lid.

Stephanie Brakespeare got sent back to the coach for sticking her head too far up a chimney.

Daniel Carrington got sent back to the coach (and seven years' bad luck) for tapping a mirror with a poker.

And then Melanie Simpson got sent back to the coach for shining her torch and then dropping it on Mrs Peters' toe when she got caught.

Which was an accident. But she still got her torch confiscated.

Jack said there was no way he wanted to risk getting his torch confiscated because he needed it for night-time shadow missions.

I said there was no way I wanted to risk getting my torch confiscated either because red, green and white are my favourite colours.

It wasn't going to happen anyway because it was lunch time and, for the next hour, all we needed to get out of our school bags were our lunches.

And our drinks. We definitely needed our drinks!

When we stepped outside, the sun was shining even brighter. PLUS the Bobbington Hall gardens were MASSIVE! You should have seen how stripy the lawns were! You should have seen how shapey the hedges were! There were hedges shaped like triangles. There were hedges shaped like balls. There were massive square flowerbeds all over the place. There were really long walls we could walk along (except Mrs Peters said we weren't allowed to). There was even a massive fountain that squirted water up into the air just like a whale!

"Anyone who hasn't been sent back to the coach," said Mrs Peters, "find a space on the lawn like ambassadors, sit down on the grass like ambassadors, open your school bags like ambassadors, take out your lunch boxes like ambassadors, chew your food like ambassadors, swallow your food like ambassadors and, if there is anything I have forgotten, do that like ambassadors too."

"I don't think she's very happy with us," said Gabby, opening her lunch box and biting into her cheese sandwich.

"We haven't done anything wrong," I said, taking one of my sandwiches out too. "It was the others who got sent back to the coach, not us."

"Only because they got caught and we didn't," said Gabby.

"How many rooms do you think Bobbington Hall has?" asked Harry, unzipping his school bag and taking out his drink and a sausage roll.

"Loads," said Jack, taking two end bits of bread out of his sandwich box, putting them together and taking a massive bite. "We haven't even been upstairs yet!"

The **trouble with putting two end bits of bread together** is I'd never seen a sandwich made like that before.

"What have you got inside your sandwich?" I asked Jack, once his first bite had eventually gone down.

"Nothing," he said.

"What, not even low-cholesterol spread?" I asked.

"Nope," said Jack. "It's part of my survival training."

"What survival training?" asked Gabby, opening a bag of prawn cocktail crisps.

"Can't say, I'm afraid," said Jack. "The kind of training I do is totally secret."

"I think Barry Morely is counting the roof tiles," said Gabby, going for a pork pie this time.

"He is SO going to win the Ambassador's Golden Cushion," said Colin, munching an apple.

"Right, I'm done," said Jack, finishing his nothing sandwich and then climbing to his feet. "Anyone fancy doing some exploring?"

The **trouble with exploring** is I wasn't sure if we were allowed to do exploring on a school trip. Not even if we explored like ambassadors. Plus I hadn't finished my lunch.

"I'm not sure Mrs Peters will let us go exploring," I said. "Plus I've still got a banana and a yoghurt to eat."

"I don't think we'll be allowed to go exploring either," said Harry. "Plus I've still got a cheese string and a doughnut to finish."

"I've still got a samosa and a jam tart," said Colin.

"I've still got my crisps, a yoghurt, a banana, some grapes and a chocolate brownie," sighed Gabby. "I wish my mum wouldn't put so much in."

"You finish your lunches, and I'll go and ask Mrs Peters if we can explore," said Jack, heading off in the direction of the fountain. "And if there's anything you can't eat, I don't mind eating it for you. IF IT HELPS!"

When Jack came back from the fountain, we knew exactly what Mrs Peters had said without him even telling us because he had taken his school bag off his shoulders.

"She said no, didn't she?" said Colin, handing Jack the last bit of his samosa.

"Yup," said Jack, popping it into his mouth.

"I knew she'd say no," said Harry, breaking his doughnut in half and giving one bit to Jack.

"Me too," I said. "You don't eat banana skins, do you, Jack?"

"Not really," he said, "although if my plane crashed in a jungle and my survival depended on it, I definitely would."

"You haven't got a plane," said Gabby, giving him her yoghurt, her grapes and her chocolate brownie.

"I will have one day," Jack said, sitting down on the grass and eating the rest of Gabby's lunch too.

"Does survival training mean you can eat other things apart from nothing sandwiches?" I asked.

"Not really," said Jack. "But after what Mrs Peters has just told me, I can promise you we are going to need all the proteins, carbohydrates, minerals and vitamins we can get."

"Why, what has she just told you?" asked Gabby.

"Yes, what has she just told you?" I asked.

"She's just told me . . ." said Jack, swallowing the last bit of chocolate brownie and then licking his fingers one by one. "She's just told me that when everyone has finished their lunches, anyone who wants to can follow her to THE MAZE!"

CHAPTER 17

The **trouble with mazes** is I'd never heard of a maze before, so I didn't exactly know what a maze was.

"I want to go to the maze," said Gabby.

"I'm definitely going to the maze," said Harry.

Almost everyone wanted to go to the maze. Including Barry Morely!

Liberty Pearce, David Alexander and Lily Hanrahan didn't, though – they wanted to stay by the fountain and try and win the Ambassador's Golden Cushion. Jasmine Smart couldn't go either because she's always really slow eating her lunch.

"A maze is one of the most dangerous places on earth," said Jack when we started lining up like ambassadors behind Mrs Peters. "It's like a death trap made of leaves."

"How do you mean?" I asked, beginning to wonder if staying by the fountain might be safer.

"Imagine a hedge," said Jack. "A really tall hedge covered in leaves, too tall to look over and too leafy to see through. Now times it by a million."

"A million?" I gasped.

"A million," repeated Jack. "Times it by a million, then join all the hedges together to create the zigzaggiest path on earth, with some hedges pointing forwards, some hedges pointing backwards, some hedges pointing left, some hedges pointing right."

"Why do the hedges point in so many different ways?" I asked.

"So you get lost," said Jack.

"Lost?" I frowned.

"LOST." Jack nodded. "Maybe FOR EVER!"

"FOR EVER?" I shuddered.

"That's right," said Jack. "Not only do mazes have loads of paths, they have loads of dead ends too. Some people have got lost in a maze for days. Some people have even died trying to find their way out."

"Is that why they call them dead ends?" I asked.

"Probably," said Jack. "The dead ends in mazes are totally designed to test your survival skills to the max."

"If you got lost in a maze for days and then got really hungry, could you eat the leaves?" I asked.

"Not if it's made of yew hedges," Jack said. "Yew hedges are totally poisonous. Especially the berries."

"I'm not really sure they should have mazes on school trips," I said.

"With my survival skills, we'll be fine," said Jack. "Just follow me."

When I told Gabby how easy it was to get lost in a maze, she said she already knew because she'd been in a maze before. Not the maze at Bobbington Hall – a different one, with her mum and dad.

"Did you find your way out?" I asked.

"Well, I'm here now, aren't I!" she laughed. "If I hadn't found my way out, I'd still be there! So would my mum and dad!!"

Once I realized that Gabby had maze experience, I began to feel much better about going inside one. Although I did think she could have saved her chocolate brownie in case of emergency, instead of giving it to Jack.

"Now then, children," said Mrs Peters when we got to a gap in a really big hedge. "Enter the maze like

ambassadors and navigate your way through the maze like ambassadors. I will be there to meet you on the other side."

The moment I realized that Mrs Peters wasn't actually coming into the maze with us, I knew it must be dangerous.

"Mrs Peters doesn't want to get lost," I whispered. "She knows how easy it is to get lost in a maze and she doesn't want to die like the rest of us."

"Stick with me," said Gabby, taking my hand and leading me in. "Stick with me and we'll be fine."

The **trouble with sticking with Gabby** is I'd already said I'd stick with Jack. Trouble is, they wanted to go different ways.

At least, I think they were different ways, because after about five minutes of going forwards, backwards, left and right, I couldn't tell which way was which.

"Have we been down here before?" Gabby asked me when we got to our fifth dead end in a row.

"I'm not really sure," I said. "It all looks really green."

"*We* have," said Jack, turning a corner and bumping into us with Harry and Colin. "I told you this place was a death trap."

"What are the leaves made of?" I asked, staring at another huge wall of green.

"They're definitely yew hedges," said Jack, "so don't even think about getting hungry."

The **trouble with not even thinking about getting hungry** is, all it makes you think about is getting hungry.

"I wish I'd brought my banana skin," I said to Gabby. "Our survival might depend on it."

"Let's go this way," she said, leading us to another dead end. "Let's go this way . . . Let's go this way . . . Let's go this way . . ." she kept saying, leading us to dead end after dead end.

"Let's ask Bernadette," I said when we bumped into B e r n a d e t t e Laine and Fiona Tucker.

"Let's ask Ollie," I said when we bumped into Oliver Cornwall and Richard Stokes.

"Let's ask the twins," I said when we bumped into Lottie and Dottie Taylor.

But it didn't matter who we bumped into –

no one knew the way out.

Apart from Barry Morely.

"Mrs Peters says we need to go back to the Hall now," he said, "so

she's asked me to come and get you."

"Did you find your way out?"
I gasped.

"Yes," said Barry.

"And all the way back in?" gasped
Gabby.

"Yes," said Barry.

"And now you can find your way

all the way back out again?" I asked.

"Yes," said Barry, "no trouble."

"Without getting lost?" I asked.

"Yes," said Barry.

"HOW?!!!" we all

asked.

"By keeping to the left," said Barry. "That's the way mazes work: if you keep turning left, eventually you'll find your way out."

"He's definitely going to win the golden cushion," whispered Gabby.

Because do you know what? Barry *did* know the way out without getting lost once!

CHAPTER 18

As soon as Mrs Peters had finished doing her headcount, we started walking back to the fountain. (Like ambassadors.)

"Imagine finding a secret passage that turned out to be a secret maze full of secret passages!" said Gabby.

"I'd hate to find a load of secret treasure and then not be able to get out!" said Harry.

"You couldn't spend the treasure," said Gabby.

"You'd be furious," said Colin.

"Not as furious as Mrs Peters is

going to be," I said, pointing over to the fountain.

The **trouble with fountains** is, if you're on a school trip, you're only meant to sit beside them. You're not meant to get in them. Especially if you're dressed in your school clothes.

But Liberty Pearce had got into the fountain dressed in her school clothes, David Alexander had got into the fountain dressed in his school clothes. So had Lily Hanrahan and Jasmine Smart.

As soon as everyone saw Liberty, David, Lily and Jasmine standing in the actual fountain, we ran full pelt (instead of like ambassadors) to see what they were doing.

"DOUBLOONS!" said Lily.

"DOUBLOONS!" said David, holding out handfuls of wet coins.

As soon as Jack, Harry and Colin realized that the fountain was full of doubloons, they jumped in too. Only Harry tripped and fell flat on his face in the water.

The **trouble with falling flat on your face in the water** is even more of your school uniform gets wet. Including your school bag.

Mrs Peters didn't jump into the fountain. Mrs Peters went absolutely doolally. In fact, she went so doolally, I can't even describe what colours her face went.

"But we've found doubloons, miss," said Jack, holding out a handful of coins too.

"Spanish doubloons," added Colin.

"THEY ARE NOT DOUBLOONS!" shouted Mrs Peters. "THEY ARE COINS,

THROWN INTO THE FOUNTAIN FOR GOOD LUCK BY VISITORS TO BOBBINGTON HALL! NOW GET OUT OF THE WATER, EMPTY YOUR POCKETS AND PUT THOSE COINS BACK WHERE YOU FOUND THEM!!!!!"

The **trouble with putting coins back where you found them** is no one really wanted to. Which meant that when they started putting them back where they'd found them, they did it really, really slowly.

Which made Mrs Peters even crosser.

"FIVE-P PIECES!" she shouted, taking all the coins out of David's pockets and throwing them back into the fountain herself. "TWO-P PIECES!" she shouted, moving on to Liberty and Colin's treasure next. "ONE-P PIECES . . . TEN-P PIECES! . . . A EURO! ANOTHER EURO! . . . A BOTTLE TOP! . . . MORE TWO-P PIECES . . . A WASHER!"

By the time everybody's treasure had gone back in the water, Mrs Peters was almost shaking.

"WHAT ON EARTH POSSESSED ANY OF YOU TO THINK THERE MIGHT BE

SPANISH DOUBLOONS IN A FOUNTAIN AT BOBBINGTON HALL?! DO I LOOK LIKE A PIRATE? IS THERE A PARROT ON MY SHOULDER? BECAUSE IF THERE IS, I CERTAINLY CAN'T SEE IT!!!"

It's OK. No one said anything.

Our secret pact was safe!

CHAPTER 19

By the time we went back inside Bobbington Hall, we only had fifteen ambassadors left. Plus Mrs Peters had sent herself back to the coach to make sure that Jack, Harry, Colin, David, Liberty, Jasmine and Lily had dried out properly before they were allowed on.

There was no sign of Mr Rowley either. Apparently he wasn't feeling very well.

"Hello," said our new olden guide when she met us at the bottom of

Bobbington Hall's massive olden staircase. "My name is Mrs Simmons. This afternoon I will be telling you about life *upstairs* at Bobbington Hall. Please follow me."

By the time we had followed Mrs Simmons to the top of the stairs, we had all agreed that it might be a good idea if we didn't look for secret passages any more.

"Agreed?" I whispered.

"AGREED," everyone whispered back.

The **trouble with agreeing not to look for secret passages any more** is we had to listen to Mrs Simmons instead:

"Behold, children! The balustrade of the main staircase at Bobbington Hall was designed and made by the Huguenot wood carver Jacques Tatti . . .

"The walls of the master bedroom are embellished with a number of Tudor carvings . . .

"The gilt table in the Queen Anne Room is late seventeenth century, while the ormolu and bronze candelabra beside the bed is French, circa 1850."

"I think I preferred the maze," whispered Gabby.

"Me too," I whispered back.

The **trouble with preferring the maze** is it made my ears stop listening to Mrs Simmons and my eyeballs start moving in other directions.

"I wonder what that rope is for," I whispered, tugging Gabby by the ponytail and pointing down a corridor that Mrs Simmons hadn't even mentioned.

"What rope?" she asked.

"*That* rope." I pointed.

The rope I had spotted was like no rope I had ever seen before. It stretched right across the corridor from wall to wall, it was redder than normal ropes, thicker than normal ropes, plus it was attached to both walls with golden hooks!

"Maybe it's an olden skipping game," said Gabby, glancing back at everyone who was still following Mrs Simmons.

"Shall we see if we can jump over it?" I whispered, tugging her into the corridor before anyone noticed we were missing.

"I'm not sure we're allowed,"

Gabby said, peeping back round the wall. "What if we get caught?"

"We won't get caught," I told her. "They've all gone through to the next room. I'm definitely going to play the olden skipping game!"

Playing the olden skipping game was loads more fun than listening to Mrs Simmons.

"My turn," said Gabby, after I'd done twelve really good skips in a row.

"I think it's more of a jumping game than a skipping game," panted Gabby after doing about twenty sideways hops over the rope and then a star jump to finish.

"You don't think this could be a secret corridor, do you?" I whispered.

"It might be," Gabby whispered back. "I mean, no one else in our class even noticed it."

"Even Mrs Simmons didn't notice it," I said. "Where do you think it leads?"

The **trouble with wondering where a secret corridor leads** is you have to go down the corridor to find out.

So we did.

"It doesn't look like it goes anywhere," said Gabby, tiptoeing further and further down the long green carpet. "It just looks like wooden panelling all the way to the end."

Gabby was right. The only thing we could see at the end of two long lines of wooden panelling was more wooden panelling.

Tiptoe by tiptoe we explored the secret corridor even further.

"What if the carpet is booby-trapped?" I whispered. "If this really is a secret corridor, it might have secret booby traps under the carpet!"

"To stop us finding the secret treasure?" whispered Gabby.

I nodded. "Exactly."

"If there's secret booby traps, they'll probably be in the middle of the carpet," whispered Gabby, pressing her back to the wall and tiptoeing as far away from the middle as she could.

"You're so right," I whispered, pressing my back to the opposite wall and inching my way further down the corridor.

"There's a door!" gasped Gabby suddenly, looking at me with really excited eyeballs.

"Where?" I asked.

"HERE!" she said, reaching out with her left hand and pointing sideways with one finger. "Can you see what I see?"

Gabby was right again. At the very end of the corridor, on the very left of the wall, totally, totally, totally disguised into the wooden panelling, was a door made of wooden panelling too!!!! If it hadn't had a doorknob, a keyhole and a sign hanging on it, we would never have known it was there!

"What does NO ADMITTANCE mean?" whispered Gabby, reading the words on the sign.

Taking my whole life in my hands, I jumped across the carpet and joined Gabby right up close to the door handle.

"I'm not sure," I said. "I know what NO means, but I think ADMITTANCE must be a very olden word."

"I know what ADMIT means," said Gabby, stroking her chin. "Maybe it's olden for NO ADMIT or NO ADMITTING."

"NO ADMITTING what?" I frowned.

"No idea," said Gabby.

"You don't think it's a secret door, do you?" I whispered, running my fingers along the panels.

"It could be!" whispered Gabby. "If it is, maybe no one at Bobbington Hall wants to admit it."

"You don't think this could be an olden secret handle on an olden secret door, leading to an olden secret passage, do you?" I whispered, putting my fingers around the doorknob.

"There's only one way to find out!" smiled Gabby.

CHAPTER 20

When I turned the olden secret handle on the olden secret door and pushed it open, our eyeballs nearly fell onto the carpet. Jack was totally right!

All we could see in front of us was total darkness. A darkness so dark and so total we hardly dared take another step forward.

"Torches at the ready," I gulped, heaving my school bag off my shoulders and unzipping the zip with trembling fingers.

The instant we switched our torch beams on, the darkness got less dark but a hundred times more creepy.

"You've got your torch on green!" whispered Gabby.

"Sorry," I said, switching it from green to red to white.

"WOH!" gasped Gabby as we got our first proper look inside.

"DOUBLE WOH!" I gasped, swinging my torch beam upwards, downwards and from side to side.

"Jack is going to be so jealous." I grinned.

"And Harry and Colin," added Gabby.

"ABSOLUTELY EVERYONE IN 4C is going to be so jealous," I said. "Including Barry Morely!"

Because – guess what? Our secret corridor hadn't just led us to a secret door. The secret door had led us to a SECRET ROOM! Not just one secret room either – a secret room that led to another secret room that led to ANOTHER SECRET ROOM!!!! AND ANOTHER!!!!!!!!!!!!!!!!!

"It's like a maze of secret rooms," whispered Gabby, tiptoeing into the darkness and pointing her torch in all directions. "You don't think we'll get lost, do you?"

"Not if we open the curtains."
I smiled.

The olden curtains in the olden secret room were really long and really heavy, but once we got them open, the sunshine came bursting in.

"It's like a really olden lounge," said Gabby, looking around at all the wooden panelling and then stroking a big leather sofa.

Gabby was kind of right and kind of wrong, because not only did the secret room have lots and lots of olden things in it – it had lots of newden things too. It even had a newden telly and a newden DVD player!

"Keep exploring," I said, resting my torch on a coffee table and heading for another secret door. "There's more to discover for sure!!"

The more secret doors we opened, the more secret things we found. Not just olden things either. Newden things as well!

We found a newden washing machine, a newden dishwasher, a newden food mixer, a newden smoothie maker, a newden toaster. We even found a newden fridge with newden-looking milk and orange juice in it.

In another room we found some newden electric toothbrushes, in another room we found a newden

digital radio, and in the smallest room there was even a newden computer!

"I wish Jack, Harry and Colin were here to see this!" I whispered. "They would be so jealous!"

"I don't," said Gabby, opening an olden drawer and then closing it really quickly.

"Why – what have you found?" I asked.

"Only papers," she said. "Nothing golden at all."

"It's a shame there are no doubloons amongst all this newden stuff," I said, shining my torch into an olden biscuit tin and actually finding some custard creams.

"Do you fancy a secret snack?" I asked. "And a glass of orange?"

"I'll tell you what." Gabby smiled. "Why don't I do the secret snacks while you choose a secret DVD for us to watch?"

It was another brilliant idea, because – guess what? Our secret room even had a newden DVD rack!

It was just like watching a DVD at home, only instead of us only being allowed one biscuit each, we could help ourselves to as many as we liked.

And crisps!

And orange juices!

"Secret rooms are the best!" said Gabby.

"Secret rooms are AWESOME!" I smiled.

At least, they were until Mrs Simmons and Mr Rowley came in.

Then went out.

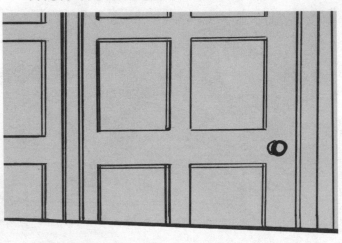

But then came back.

With Mrs Peters.

When Mrs Peters found us on the secret sofa in our secret room eating secret crisps and drinking secret juice, she was so angry she couldn't speak. Her mouth just kept going up and down without any words actually coming out.

They did come out eventually, but we were on the coach going home by then.

And we were down to thirteen ambassadors.

CHAPTER 21

When I told Jack that me and Gabby had actually found secret rooms at the end of a secret corridor in Bobbington Hall, he said they weren't secret rooms at all. They were the rooms where the owners of Bobbington Hall actually lived. That's why the corridor had a rope across it.

Trouble is, then things got worse. Because according to Harry and Colin, a search party had been out looking for us all afternoon.

They'd looked in the Hall, they'd

looked in the gardens, they'd even looked for us in the fountain!

Double trouble is, Mrs Peters and Miss Fletcher got lost looking for us in the maze, which meant that another search party had to be sent out. Only there wasn't anyone else left in Bobbington Hall to join the search.

So a police car had to come and look for us as well.

And all the gardeners.

And a man on a bike who was delivering leaflets.

But no one could find us anywhere.

So a police helicopter had to come and look for us as well.

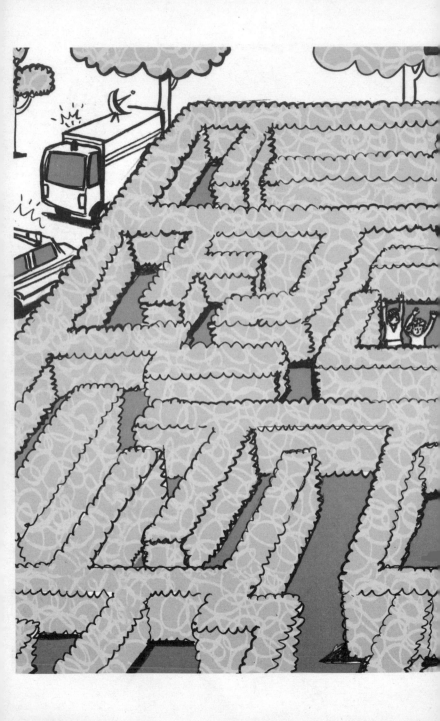

How me and Gabby were meant to know that the owners of Bobbington Hall actually lived in the secret rooms we had found I really do not know. Their front door didn't look anything like a proper front door. It didn't have a letterbox. It didn't have a doorbell. It didn't even have a house number on it! All it had on it was wooden panels and a sign that didn't make sense.

WHICH ABSOLUTELY, TOTALLY, WASN'T OUR FAULT!

Tomorrow morning, me, Gabby, Jack, Harry, Colin, Melanie, Vicky, Liberty, Jasmine, Sanjay, Liam, David, Chelsea, Stephanie, Lily and both Daniels have got to go and see Mr Copford, our headmaster. I think he wants to talk to us about how ambassadors should behave on a school trip.

Oh well, at least Mrs Peters marked all our worksheets while we were driving back to school.

Which means . . .

Wait for it . . .

That's right . . .

GABBY AND I BOTH WON THE

AMBASSADOR'S GOLDEN CUSHION!

Because no one in our entire class apart from us got 50 out of 50 answers right!!

Not even Barry Morely!

(Barry nearly did, but he was one roof tile out.)

P.S. In case you're wondering, Gabby found the answers in that secret drawer!

DAISY'S
TROUBLE
INDEX

The trouble with . . .

More than a million

DAISY

books sold!

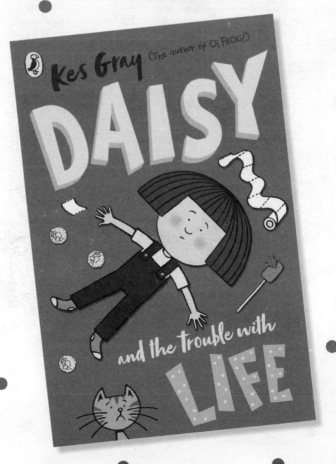

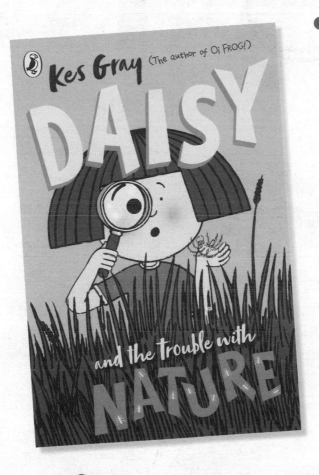

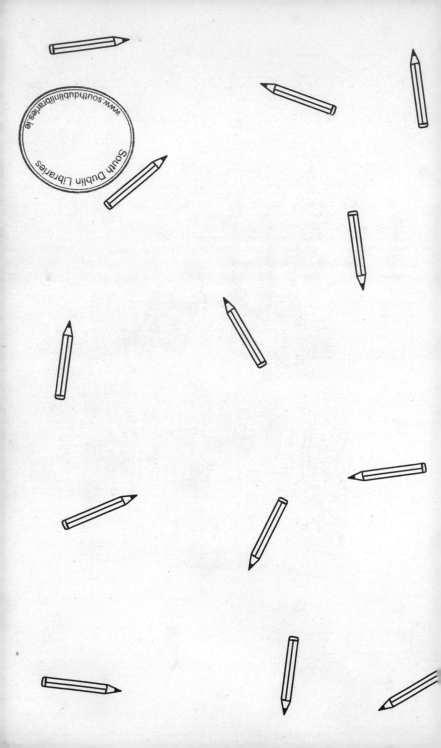